All about...

Michael Morpurgo

Heinemann
LIBRARY

Shaun McCarthy

www.heinemann.co.uk/library

Visit our website to find out more information about **Heinemann Library** books.

To order:

☎ Phone 44 (0) 1865 888066

🖹 Send a fax to 44 (0) 1865 314091

💻 Visit the Heinemann Bookshop at www.heinemann.co.uk/library to browse our catalogue and order online.

First published in Great Britain by Heinemann Library, Halley Court, Jordan Hill, Oxford OX2 8EJ, part of Harcourt Education. Heinemann is a registered trademark of Harcourt Education Ltd.

Editorial: Lucy Thunder and Helen Cannons
Design: David Poole and Geoff Ward
Picture Research: Rebecca Sodergren and Kay Altwegg
Production: Edward Moore

Originated by Repro Multi-Warna
Printed and bound in China by South China Printing Company.
The paper used to print this book comes from sustainable resources.

ISBN 0 431 17985 9
08 07 06 05 04
10 9 8 7 6 5 4 3 2 1

British Library Cataloguing in Publication Data
McCarthy, Shaun
All about Michael Morpurgo
823.9′14
A full catalogue record for this book is available from the British Library.

Acknowledgements
The Publishers would like to thank the following for permission to reproduce photographs:
Collections p**24**; Corbis / James Davis p**13**; Corbis / Brian Harding: Eye Ubiquitous p**10**; Egmont Books Ltd pp**15**, **29**; 1997 & 2002 Michael Foreman / Egmont Books Ltd p**23**; Chris Honeywell p**4**; Hulton Archive pp**6**, **8**, **9**, **16**; Michael Morpurgo pp**7**, **11**, **14**, **18**, **21**, **22**, **26**, **27**, **28**; Sylvia Palmer / Michael Morpurgo p**20**; Topfoto pp**5**, **19**; Patrick Ward / Corbis p**12**; Topham Picturepoint / Pressnet p**25**.

Cover photograph of Michael Morpurgo at a book signing in 2003, reproduced with permission of Tudor Photography.

Sources
The author and Publishers gratefully acknowledge the publications which were used for research and as written sources for this book:

Telling Tales: An Interview with Michael Morpurgo (Mammoth Books, 1999) **8**, **10**, **12**, **21**, **26**
Achuka website – www.achuka.com **28**
Collins Education website – www.collinseducation.com **25**
Farms for City Children – www.farmsforcitychildren.co.uk **22**
The *Guardian's* books website – www.books.guardian.co.uk **22**

Fiction works by Michael Morpurgo are cited in the text.

Contents

Any words appearing in the text in bold, **like this**, are explained in the glossary.

The author and Publishers would like to thank Michael Morpurgo for his invaluable help in the writing of this book.

Who is Michael Morpurgo?

Michael Morpurgo is a children's writer who has written over 90 books for young people. As well as being a very successful author, he has set up a **charity** that runs farms for city children to visit, so they can experience country life. He lives in Devon, near to one of the farms that the charity runs. It is not surprising that many of his best-loved books are about animals, and the relationships that can develop between animals and humans.

Kings, saints and ghosts

Michael has written books about lots of other subjects too: Joan of Arc, Robin Hood, King Arthur and the ghost of Sir Walter Raleigh. Some of his books tell serious, often sad, stories – like *Warhorse*, about a horse sold to the army in **World War I**. Other books, especially those for younger readers – like the *Mudpuddle Farm* series – are full of fun.

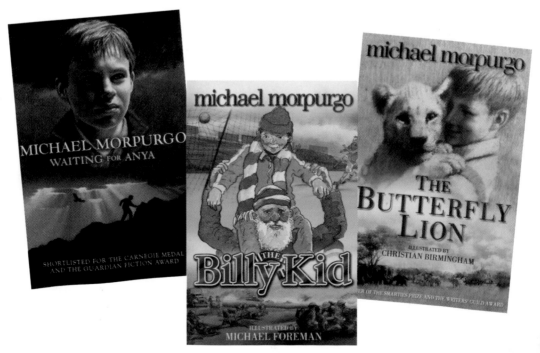

▲ Michael has written many books for children. Here is a selection of some of them.

Prizes and praise

Michael's books have won many awards, including the Whitbread Award and the Smarties Book Prize. But just as important to Michael as prizes are the comments of his readers.

One father and son left this comment on a bookshop website: 'Now we have read *Kensuke's Kingdom* we are reading all the other Michael Morpurgo books, which are all just as gripping and beautifully written.' Michael's great books appeal to readers of all ages the world over.

▲ Michael Morpurgo, the famous writer.

Factfile

★ Date of birth	5 October 1943
★ Star sign	Libra
★ Eye colour	Blue
★ Hair colour	Fair, but not much of it now!
★ Pets	A dog, a lurcher called Bercelet, and four bantam hens
★ Hobbies	Dreaming
★ Favourite food	Scilly potatoes (potatoes grown on the Scilly Isles off Cornwall)
★ Favourite childhood book	*Just So Stories* by Rudyard Kipling
★ Bad habit	Watching too much television
★ Personal motto	'Keep right on to the end of the road'

Family life

Michael was born in 1943 in St Albans, a town outside London. He was born during **World War II**. Michael's family usually lived in the middle of London, but had left to escape the German bombing raids. Thousands of bombs were dropped on the city and many people were killed. Michael's parents had both been actors and met while working in a theatre in Canterbury. Michael's father was away fighting in the army when his son was born.

A new family

When Michael was still a baby his mother met another man and fell in love. She **divorced** Michael's father and married this new man, Jack Morpurgo.

Jack brought up Michael and his older brother, Pieter as if they were his own children. In the end there were four children in this new family. Michael remembers it as a happy family when he was young, though he admits there were arguments between him and his step-brother and sister when he was young. They now get on well.

▲ The Marlowe Theatre in Canterbury, where Michael's parents met.

Dad on television

Michael's real father was called Tony Bridge. After the war he went to work as an actor in Canada. Michael was in his twenties before he met and made friends with him. But he did once see him in a film on television! It was a surprise he later used in a story called *My Father is a Polar Bear*.

▲ Michael, aged nine, at Christmas in 1952.

What Michael says

This is how Michael describes his unexpected surprise whilst watching television:

'*I was a teenager, watching the film* Great Expectations *on television at Christmas with my brother, step-brother and sister, mother and step-father and some cousins. We got to the terrifying bit where Pip (a young boy) is in the graveyard and the escaped convict, the hideous Magwitch, looms up from behind the tombstone.*
"*Oh my god,*" *said my mother, pointing at the screen.*
"*That's your father!*"'

Off to school

When **World War II** ended in 1945, Michael's family moved to Earls Court, in London. There were many bomb sites in the streets around them, where buildings had been blown up by German bomber pilots and the ruins had not been cleared away. There was one right next to Michael's school playground.

Food was still in short supply. Michael remembers going to the shops with a **ration book** to get the family's small allowance of butter.

People lived with the ruins of war for many years after World War II ended. In London, many buildings were blown up.

Fog and monks!

In the 1940s London suffered from smogs (periods of fog caused by smoke from open fires). Really bad ones were called 'pea soupers', because the air was thick and green like pea soup. Michael once walked to school in a 'pea souper' that was so thick he could not see across the road.

Michael's first school was in a gloomy old building shared with **Greek Orthodox monks**. He remembers their 'black clad figures flitting around the place'. He thought the school was 'interesting' rather than scary.

▲ Dinner time at a boarding school in 1954. Children sent away to boarding school, as Michael was, can be very lonely.

Sent away to school

After a few years, the Morpurgo family left London and moved to Bradwell-on-Sea in Essex. Michael, who was only seven, was sent away to a **boarding school** in Sussex, over 80 miles away from Bradwell-on-Sea. His older brother Pieter was already there.

Life in a boarding school was tough and Michael was **homesick**. All the boys slept together in a big room called a dormitory – there was no privacy at all. Anyone caught out of bed after lights out was caned (beaten with a stick) by a teacher. Michael says he can still hear in his mind the cries of boys being beaten. He 'got by' by being good at sports, especially cricket and rugby.

Boarding-school memories

Michael uses his memories of boarding school in his book *The War of Jenkins Ear*. The main character, Toby, is homesick, and the school is a tough place to live. Then a new friendship makes Toby's life much more exciting. In the book there is fighting between boys from the school and boys from the nearby village. Michael says there were arguments between boys in the boarding school he went to and local youngsters.

Games and books

Michael says that he was just about average in most lessons, but he became very good at games. Private boarding schools like the one Michael went to were very keen on sports. Michael was soon in the school rugby and cricket teams. He also remembers that he was good at playing marbles with his friends!

In his free time after lessons, Michael read a lot. He liked reading **biographies** of people,

▲ Canterbury Cathedral, where pupils from King's School sang.

such as famous generals and explorers. He also enjoyed poetry, but mostly when it was read aloud. Michael says the only **novels** and plays he read at school were the ones he had to read in class. *Treasure Island* by Robert Louis Stevenson was his favourite book. He hated Shakespeare!

What Michael says

Michael remembers King's as a marvellous school:

'There was lots of music. We sang in the cathedral and the school had an orchestra. It left me with a love of music. But I went for the easy options – sports and games. And I was made Captain of School, which meant I got to wear a purple gown.'

A better school

When he was thirteen Michael sat an examination for a **scholarship** to King's School, a famous and very old school in Canterbury in Kent. He passed. He admits 'I wasn't particularly brainy, but I got in for being "a jolly good all-round sort of chap".'

Michael found King's a very different sort of school, which he liked far more than the one he had been to in Sussex. Although he was still a boarder (a pupil living in the school during term time), he was much happier there.

Michael was an **officer** in the school **cadet** corps, which gave pupils a taste of what life was like in the army. He enjoyed it, and was made Company Sergeant Major, an important rank. He was also made 'Captain of School', which meant he had to meet special visitors and represent the school pupils. On his last day at school he met the **Queen Mother**, who was visiting.

▲ Michael the sportsman, far right, in King's School rugby team in 1962.

Michael the soldier

When he was eighteen Michael suddenly realized he had gone right through school without ever thinking about what he might do when he left! He decided to try the army. He won a **scholarship** to Sandhurst Military Academy, a place for training young army officers. He started there in the autumn of 1962.

Tough training

Michael arrived at Sandhurst and got the shock of his young life. His hair was hacked off, he was dressed in fatigues (plainest army uniform) and put straight into tough infantry training. As well as learning skills such as map-reading, in a classroom, the **cadets** had orders shouted at them by terrifying sergeant majors. They were made to march up and down the parade ground for hours. They trained on assault courses and did long cross-country marches carrying all their equipment. Michael said 'I knew I didn't want to spend the rest of my life in the army.'

▲ Here Sandhurst cadets are shown marching on parade.

A cunning plan!

In the summer of 1962, just before he started his training at Sandhurst, Michael had met a girl called Clare, while on holiday in Corfu in Greece. They had kept on seeing each other and had fallen in love. Although Michael was only nineteen, they wanted to marry. But marriage was not allowed for Sandhurst cadets.

Michael's mother hatched a plan. She sent a **telegram** to Sandhurst saying: 'Mother dangerously ill. Come immediately.' Of course she was perfectly well, but it gave Michael a chance to get away from Sandhurst and marry Clare in London. After a short honeymoon, Michael went back to Sandhurst and told them what he had done. Within 24 hours he was ordered out of the army.

Corfu, the Greek island where Michael met his future wife. This was a very different place from Sandhurst Military Academy!

A young father

Soon after they were married, Michael and Clare became parents. Their son Sebastian was born in 1964 when Michael was just twenty. Michael considers himself 'very lucky' to have always had children in his life. He says, 'For all my adult life children have been at the centre of my existence.'

▲ Michael and Clare, soon after they were married.

Time to study

Michael now had to support his family. In 1964 they moved to London. He managed to get a job teaching in a private school, but he knew he had to get proper qualifications if he wanted to go on and get better teaching jobs.

He studied French, English and **philosophy** at King's College in London. Then he went on to do a teaching course. He was a full-time student for three years. Clare did some teaching, too, in a private school, but by the end of Michael's course at college she was expecting their second child.

Trouble at school

Michael got a job teaching at an independent (private) school. It was ruled by a very old-fashioned head teacher who thought that children expressing their own ideas was a dangerous thing. Michael was so unhappy about the way this school treated its pupils that he made an official complaint about boys being beaten as punishment. Soon afterwards Michael resigned and took a job in a primary school in Kent, where things such as beatings did not go on!

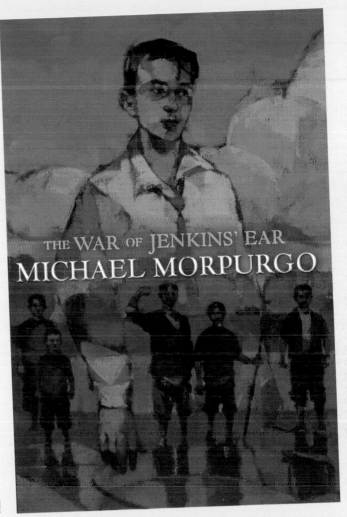

THE WAR OF JENKINS' EAR
MICHAEL MORPURGO

▲ This is one of Michael's most popular books, about a boy at **boarding school**. The school and its head teacher are based on Michael's experiences in his first job.

A very important book

Around this time, Michael read a book by the poet Ted Hughes called *Poetry in the Making*. It was about encouraging young people to express themselves through writing poetry. Michael thought it was full of wonderful ideas. It encouraged him to start thinking about writing stories himself.

The big break

Michael wrote his first stories for children when he was a teacher. He enjoyed telling stories in class, and decided he wanted to write some of his own. He showed a few ideas he had to a friend. The friend suggested Michael should write out the stories and send them to a book **publisher**. He wrote two, sent them off and waited anxiously to hear what the publisher thought. The publisher liked them and said he should write a **novel**.

So Michael began writing *Long Way Home*, about a boy called George who is sent to live with new **foster parents** on a farm. In 1975 it was published. This was his big break as a writer.

▲ Many German planes were shot down in Britain during World War II. Sometimes the crew, the 'enemy', survived. In *Friend or Foe*, the book Michael wrote after *Long Way Home*, he used this idea as the starting point for a gripping story.

Researching wars

A writer needs to do research into their subject before they begin telling the story. The subject of war and how it affects our lives is one that Michael has used in many of his books, such as *Billy the Kid* and *Kensuke's Kingdom*. He has read many books about **World Wars I and II**, and spoken with people who were involved in them.

Airmen and animals

Michael's publishers encouraged him to write more. His next book, *Friend or Foe*, was published in 1977. Set during **World War II**, it is about a German airman who saves a British boy from drowning, then asks for help in return. Readers really liked the story, and this became his first successful book.

Michael found that he had lots of stories to tell that people wanted to read, especially stories featuring animals. He wrote *The Nine Lives of Montezuma*, about a cat, *Tom's Sausage Lion* and *The White Horse of Zennor*. He would teach during the day and write in the evenings and school holidays. This way of life was hard work but Michael enjoyed the teaching and his writing.

What Michael says

Children inspired Michael to start writing:

'I began to write when I was a teacher, inspired by the fresh, spontaneous, positive way the children reacted to books I read them in class. That made me read more, and gradually I started to write my own stories.'

A growing family

By the middle of the 1970s, Michael and Clare had another young son, called Horatio, and a daughter, Rosalind. Clare was still teaching, but both she and Michael felt they wanted to work with children in other ways than teaching in schools. They wanted to stop so many children feeling like they had 'failed' at school, and to help them do things that had nothing to do with lessons and exams.

Farms For City Children

Clare's father was Sir Allen Lane, one of the most successful book publishers of the 20th century. He had started the famous Penguin Books company in 1935. When he died in 1970, Michael and Clare decided they could use some of the money he had left Clare to do something really special for children.

▲ Nethercott Farm, showing the house where visiting school parties live while they work at looking after the animals.

Let's be farmers!

After lots of thought the Morpurgos decided they wanted to set up a farm in the country where children from inner-city schools could visit. They would give up their teaching jobs and do all the jobs that need to be done on a farm themselves, including caring for the animals.

They decided that the farm would have to be set up as a **charity**, which is a very complex business, and that Michael would carry on writing books.

Nethercott Farm

In 1974 Michael and Clare went to Devon, where Clare had spent holidays with her father. They found Nethercott Farm, which was for sale. They bought it, and then spent a couple of years getting it ready for children to visit. Their country neighbours gave them all sorts of help and advice.

▲ The poet Ted Hughes was Michael's neighbour. Michael first met him in 1976.

A poet for a neighbour

One of Michael and Clare's neighbours was the famous poet Ted Hughes. He was one of the best-known poets in Britain. Like Michael, he wrote a lot about animals. It was he who had written the book *Poetry in the Making* that had inspired Michael when he was a teacher. Michael and Ted became close friends. They wrote a book together called *All Around the Year* about the changes that happen in the countryside through the four seasons. Ted Hughes died in 1998.

'Nuggets of truth'

The first school party arrived at Nethercott Farm in 1976. Many of the children had never seen a cow or a chicken. Although Michael was busy in his new role as director of the children's farm **charity**, he was also thinking about writing new stories.

Going to feed the animals on
◀ Nethercott Farm.

Warhorse

One of Michael's best-loved books was **published** in 1981. It is called *Warhorse* and tells the story of a farm horse sold to the army in **World War I**. It is a tough but beautifully written story. Michael says he was inspired to write it when he saw terrifying pictures of horses having to charge towards the barbed wire on the battlefields during World War I.

Michael did lots of research for *Warhorse*. He spoke with people in his village who could remember horses from the local farms being sent off to the war. He says it was 'tremendously exciting, like detective work. I learned a lot.' *Warhorse* was so popular with readers that in 1998 Michael wrote *Farm Boy*, another story about the same horse.

Michael enjoys meeting city children
when they first arrive at the farm.

*'One thing that always amazes them is the darkness.
They experience for the first time the pitch blackness of the
countryside ... And there was a boy who couldn't get over
feeling the stones in the earth through the soles of his
wellies. He'd only ever walked on asphalt and
concrete before!'*

Real-life ideas

More new books quickly followed *Warhorse's* success: *Twist of
Gold, Little Foxes, Jojo The Melon Donkey* and the *Mudpuddle
Farm* series for younger readers. Many of the stories featured
animals and many of Michael's ideas came from his life on the farm. He was surrounded by children and animals, just the sort of characters he creates and writes about so well. As Michael says, 'There's always a nugget of truth at the centre of each of my stories, incidents in my own life, people I've met, articles snipped out of newspapers.'

Michael at home on the farm with
his spaniel, Sophie, in 1980.

A very busy writer

The farm Michael and Clare had set up was very successful. There was lots to do on it. Michael was also writing books and getting them **published**. It was a very busy life.

School parties came to Nethercott Farm every week during term time. Michael would work with the children, showing them how to feed animals, clean out their pens and do all sorts of other farm jobs, often very mucky ones! It was very hard work, but both he and Clare were doing something they really believed in.

More farms

Throughout the 1980s, interest in Farms For City Children kept growing. The **charity** employed people to help with the school parties at Nethercott. So many schools wanted 'a week in the country' that the charity bought two more farms, one in Gloucestershire with rare breeds of animals, and one in West Wales overlooking the sea. Between them, the three farms can be visited by over 3000 children every year.

▲ Wick Court, Gloucestershire, one of the three farms run by Farms For City Children.

▲ An illustration from *Arthur, High King of Britain*. The dog looks a lot like Michael's own pet dog, Bercelet!

Stories from history

Michael rewrote stories he had already begun when he could find time between farm jobs. He would start writing new books in the school holidays. He was always looking for new subjects to write about. He often used ideas from history to create gripping stories. *My Friend Walter* (1988) was an exciting tale about the ghost of Sir Walter Raleigh. *Arthur, High King of Britain* (1994) was a retelling of the legends of King Arthur and the Knights of the round table. Michael wrote the story as though Arthur himself was describing the things that were happening in his kingdom.

He also wrote a collection of ten ghost stories, each one set in a real old house or castle owned by the National Trust. The Trust open all their properties to the public, so you can visit the place where each story is set.

Books on TV
My Friend Walter was adapted for television in 1990. Michael worked on the screenplay, helping to turn the stories into scripts that could then be read by actors. Michael loves going to the cinema, though he says he watches 'too much television'!

Mysterious island

One summer, Michael and Clare visited the Scilly Isles, the small islands off Land's End at the very tip of Cornwall. It was the first of many summer visits they have made to the islands. Michael found the Scilly Isles a very special place, and they inspired him to write stories set there.

Whales and shipwrecks

His first book written about the islands was *Why the Whales Came* (1985). It was set in the same period as *Warhorse*, during **World War I**, but was a very different sort of story, full of the mystery and superstitions of the islands. *Why the Whales Came* was made into a film in 1989.

Michael's best-known book set in the Scilly Isles is *The Wreck of the Zanzibar*. This is a tough story of life on the islands, seen through the eyes of a young girl called Laura, living there in 1907. It won several major awards for children's writing, including the Whitbread Award in 1995.

▲ The Scilly Isles, that inspired Michael to write *The Wreck of the Zanzibar.*

Working together

Michael has a rather unusual way of making different versions of a story to get it just right. He writes his first copy out on paper, very quickly. Then he sends this from Devon to a friend on the Scilly Isles who types it up on a computer. She prints a copy and sends it back to Michael. He works on this, makes lots of changes, then sends it back to be typed again. The story goes backwards and forwards until Michael thinks it is finished and ready for publishing as a book.

Many of Michael's books are also beautifully illustrated. He likes working with different illustrators to get exactly the right sort of pictures for each book.

▲ Gigs are long, heavy rowing boats used in the Scilly Isles. This is the sort of boat that Laura rows in *The Wreck of the Zanzibar*.

Michael Morpurgo on Michael Morpurgo

M ichael has given many interviews. Here are some of his answers to questions he has been asked.

Where do you write?
'I do most of my writing on the bed. I go upstairs after breakfast and sit on the bed with lots of pillows, and the book propped on my knees. Sitting at a desk gives me backache. Yes, I do get blobs of ink on the sheets … Once I've started I write very quickly, something I had to do when there was such a lot to be done on the farm and we didn't have as much help as we have now.'

How exactly do you write?
'I write longhand (full words, rather than using abbreviations or symbols), in very small handwriting, with a very fine pen on the lined pages of school exercise books. No paragraphs. I try to get as much as I can on one page, because I hate turning over and seeing a blank page.'

▲ Michael at home working on a story.

Do you do book signings in shops?
'Yes. My first public book signing was 25 years ago. I was sharing the day with another children's writer, the Reverend Awdry (who wrote *Thomas the Tank Engine* and other famous railway stories). I signed two books. The Reverend Awdry had a queue of children going right out to the street.'

Do you enjoy visiting schools?
'Yes. I have a favourite school where I often launch a new book when it comes out – St Joseph's School in Highgate, London. The children there love reading – and so do the teachers!'

▲ Michael enjoys meeting young fans like these and signing their books.

Of all the books you've written, which is your favourite?
'I suppose *Farm Boy* is my favourite book. I love the relationship in it between grandfather and grandson, perhaps because I'm a grandfather now. I love the trust built between them. I loved inventing his language, hearing all the Devon voices I've known in my head as I wrote.'

Less farming, more writing

Michael believes that children's writers should have the same kind of recognition as other authors. Being someone who puts ideas into action, in 1998 he set up the Children's Laureate award. This is a £10,000 prize given to a writer or illustrator who has produced great work for children. The first award was made to an illustrator, Quentin Blake. Writer Anne Fine was the second Children's Laureate in 2000. (Anne has written many books, including *Madame Doubtfire*.) In 2003 the group of people who decide who should become the Laureate chose Michael himself. This was because his writing is so popular and so valuable in children's lives.

▲ Michael and Clare with their MBEs in 1999.

Award for charity work

In 1999 Michael and Clare were each awarded an MBE (Member of the British Empire) for setting up Farms For City Children. The **charity** is still as successful as ever, and the farms are just as busy. Michael now does less work on the farm in Devon himself. He is concentrating on writing his books.

Boy overboard

Michael is interested in writing about relationships between young people and adults. In 1999 he wrote *Kensuke's Kingdom*. The main character is a boy leading an ordinary life, until his parents buy a yacht and sail round the world. The boy is washed overboard. He struggles to an island where he meets a Japanese soldier who has lived alone there for 40 years. The friendship that develops between them creates a wonderful and moving story.

What Michael says

Michael has this to say about his writing:

'When I write I don't pretend. When I'm feeling serious I will write on serious topics, and when I feel silly I do silly stuff!'

Keeping his fans happy

Michael knows he has many young fans who wait for each new book to come out. As a hard-working writer, and a man who has always been involved with children – including his own – he is not going to let them down. Watch out for many more Michael Morpurgo books to come.

Michael Morpurgo
Kensuke's Kingdom

With illustrations by Michael Foreman

FCBG
Winner
The Children's
Book Award
2000

▲ *Kensuke's Kingdom* is one of Michael's most popular books.

Timeline

1943 Michael Morpurgo is born in St Albans, Hertfordshire
1962 Begins training to be an army officer (and quickly leaves!)
1963 Marries Clare Lane
1964–1967 Trains to be a teacher
1974 Buys Nethercott Farm and starts a **charity** – Farms For City Children
1975 *Long Way Home* is **published**
1982 *Warhorse*, his first best-seller, is published
1998 Sets up the Children's **Laureate** award to celebrate good books for young people
1999 *Kensuke's Kingdom* is published
2003 Michael is made Children's Laureate

Books by Michael Morpurgo

Here are some books by Michael you might like to read:

Warhorse (Egmont, 1982)
> Joey the horse is sold to the Army in **World War I** and is sent from his Devon farm to the battlefields of France.

Why the Whales Came (Egmont, 1985)
> A tale of mystery that starts with a whale being washed up onto the Scilly Isles.

Farm Boy (Collins, 1998)
> The 'follow-up' to *Warhorse*, about what happens when the horse goes back to the farm after the war.

Kensuke's Kingdom (Egmont, 1999)
> A young English boy and an ex-Japanese soldier find themselves sharing a desert island and have to learn to live together.

Glossary

biography book written about someone's life (by someone else)

boarding school school where pupils stay and live during term-time

cadet young trainee soldier

charity organization set up to help people

divorce legal process for ending a marriage

foster parents people acting as parents to children whose real parents are unable to take care of them

Greek Orthodox form of Christianity practised mainly in Greece

homesick missing home and family very much

Laureate title given to writers for their good work

monk religious man who gives up normal life to devote himself to prayer and to helping others

novel book-length story

officer person in the army who is in charge of other soldiers

philosophy study of what reality is, and how people can know it

publish to produce and sell books. A company that publishes books is called a publisher.

Queen Mother mother of Queen Elizabeth II. The Queen Mother died in 2002.

ration book a book of coupons used to be exchanged for certain foods during World War II

scholarship award of money used to pay fees. To get this, a pupil passes a special examination to get into a private school or college.

telegram very short letter used to send urgent messages

World War I war that lasted from 1914–1918, it was fought throughout Europe. It is sometimes known as the Great War.

World War II war that lasted from 1939 to 1945. It began when Germany marched its army into Poland.

Index

Titles in the *All About Authors* series are:

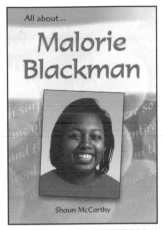

All about...
Malorie Blackman

Shaun McCarthy

Hardback   0 431 17982 4

All about...
Rob Childs

Shaun McCarthy

Hardback   0 431 17986 7

All about...
Roald Dahl

Vic Parker

Hardback   0 431 17981 6

All about...
Anne Fine

Vic Parker

Hardback   0 431 17987 5

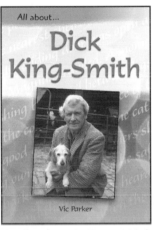

All about...
Dick King-Smith

Vic Parker

Hardback   0 431 17988 3

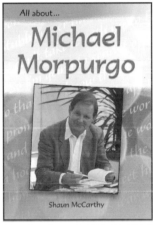

All about...
Michael Morpurgo

Shaun McCarthy

Hardback   0 431 17985 9

All about...
J.K. Rowling

Shaun McCarthy

Hardback   0 431 17980 8

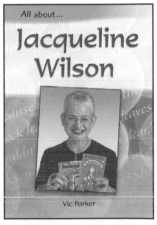

All about...
Jacqueline Wilson

Vic Parker

Hardback   0 431 17983 2

Find out about the other titles in this series on our website www.heinemann.co.uk/library